MOMMY THE SUN
IS POINTING AT ME

MOMMY THE SUN IS POINTING AT ME
by
Ruth Gadson-Smith and Adam Smith

Illustrations by Kerry James

Published by

Khocolate Keepsakes Children's Museum

2808 West Florence Avenue, Los Angeles, CA 90043

First Printing 2017

Printed in the United States of America

Design Layout Lorriane Dean

Illustrations by Kerry James and Yannet Gastelum

Library of Congress cataloging in publication data:

Smith-Gadson, Ruth

Smith, Adam

MOMMY THE SUN IS POINTING AT ME

ISBN 978-1548702878

Introduction

Adam was three years-old in August 2016 when he inspired me to write our first children's book. As we traveled from Atlanta, Georgia through the mountains of Kentucky on our way to visit family in Ohio, he sat in his car seat. Gazing out of the window, he said to me, "Mommy, the sun is pointing at me." Those seven words prompted an entire conversation about the sun and why it was "pointing" at him.

As I continued driving, I dictated to my mother the words that Adam had spoken, and she promptly wrote them down on the back of a receipt. From there the idea blossomed about writing a book based on our conversation. Adam's personification of the sun brought forth the idea of bringing this book to life---as it explores how much fun our friend, the sun, can be!

Acknowledgements

R.G.S.-- My heartfelt thanks and appreciation go to my very dear friend, mentor and sorority sister, Carliss R. McGhee Ph.D., without whom this book would have remained scribbled on the back of an old receipt in my purse. Big "thank yous" to my illustrators Kerry James and Yannet Gastelum, as well as to my graphic designer Lorraine Dean. Sincere appreciation to my editor Denise Bertrand, and to Khocolate Keepsakes for publishing my first book. My deepest gratitude goes to my mother, Rose Gadson, who on a hot August day took the time to write as I dictated the book to her--while I drove through the Appalachian Mountains of Kentucky, on Interstate 75.
.

A.S.--Thank you to my mommy, and my Grammy, who did not dismiss my banter about the sun on that extremely hot day in August 2016. And thank you to my brother and sister, who rode silently in the car next to me and did not interrupt me.

Dedication

Ruth: Dedicated to my children Ashley, Caleb, and Adam. My husband, John, and my mom, Rose.

Adam: Dedicated to Mommy, Daddy, Ashley, Caleb, Grammy and all of my friends.

Mommy, the sun is pointing at me.

He is pointing at you from high in the sky because he thinks you are a great little guy.

Mommy, the sun is following me.

He is following you from high in the sky, bouncing and laughing, because you are a cool guy.

Mommy, the sun is chasing me.

He is chasing you from high in the sky--running, jumping and shouting--zip boom bah!

Mommy, the sun is hiding from me.

He is hiding from you!

From way up, high behind the clouds he--peeks out again--because he thinks that you are a great friend.

Mommy, the
sun is going
away.

He is going
away; down,
down, from the
sky because it is
time
to say good
bye.

ABOUT THE AUTHOR

Adam Smith

Four-year-old Adam was born in Okinawa, Japan, where he lives with his Mom, Dad, brother, sister and his Grammy. He enjoys running, laughing and joking with his family. He also loves playing video games with his big brother, Caleb, and racing his matchbox cars. Adam attends Eiko-Yochien, a Japanese preschool and kindergarten.

ABOUT THE AUTHOR

RUTH GADSON-SMITH

Ruth Gadson-Smith enjoys traveling and eating new foods, reading novels and spending time with her family. She was born in Fayetteville, NC, but lived as a military brat all over the U.S. and in Würzburg, Germany. She is currently a high school Language Arts and AVID teacher for the Department of Defense Dependent Schools in Okinawa, Japan, and is a mother to three delightfully-spirited children. She is a Howard University graduate, a member of Delta Sigma Theta Sorority, Inc., and is married to her Coleman-Love, John Smith, a member of Omega Psi Phi Fraternity, Inc.

Made in the USA
Columbia, SC
18 January 2021